COLLEGE SPORTS TODAY

COLLEGE SPORTS TODAY

FIGHT ON!

THE USC TROJANS STORY

ERIC BRAUN

CREATIVE EDUCATION

Published by Creative Education
123 South Broad Street, Mankato, Minnesota 56001
Creative Education is an imprint of The Creative Company

Designed by Stephanie Blumenthal
Production design by The Design Lab
Editorial assistance by John Nichols

Photos by: Allsport USA, AP/Wide World Photos,
SportsChrome, UPI/Corbis-Bettmann, and Archive Photos

Library of Congress Cataloging-in-Publication Data

Braun, Eric, 1971–
Fight on! the USC Trojans story / by Eric Braun.
p. cm. — (College football today)
Summary: Highlights some of the important personalities and key moments in
football played at the University of Southern California.
ISBN: 0-88682-985-2

1. University of Southern California—Football—History—Juvenile literature. 2. Southern California Trojans
(Football team)—History—Juvenile literature. [1. Southern California Trojans (Football team)—History.
2. Football—History.] I. Title. II. Series: College football today (Mankato, Minn.)

GV958.U57B74   1999
796.332'63'0979494—dc21   98-35316

First Edition

2 4 6 8 9 7 5 3 1

"BEWARE THE MEN OF TROY!"

SINCE 1912, THE

TROJANS HAVE STRUCK

FEAR INTO OPPONENTS.

Across oceans of time, this warning cry has shaken the courage of the bravest of men. From the ancient Greeks to the modern Cornhuskers, facing fierce Trojan warriors on the field of battle has meant that a fearsome beating is almost assured. Although the legendary men of Troy were ultimately undone by the Greeks and their Trojan Horse, today's University of Southern California (USC) football Trojans continue the fight on the grid-iron. For more than 110 years, USC has been one of the most dominant football programs in the country. With a glorious history that includes eight national championships, 40 bowl appearances, and four Heisman Trophy winners, these modern-day men of Troy continue to strike fear into the hearts of opponents everywhere.

BUILDING A WINNER

In the 1870s, when Los Angeles was nothing more than a frontier town with no paved streets, electric lights, or telephones, the town's ambitious leaders were eager to start building it into a better place. One of these leaders was Judge Robert Maclay Widney, who founded the University of Southern California in 1880.

The university grew steadily until 1887, when it was hit with money troubles and nearly collapsed. In spite of its financial woes, USC fielded its first football team in 1888 and went 2–0 for two straight years behind quarterback Arthur Carroll, who also tailored the players' pants. In the four wins, the team outscored its opponents by a total of 86–0. Although the school had no football team for two of the following three years, a precedent had been set.

The hard work and dedication that was needed to simply bring a USC team into existence would be evident in the school's sports teams for years to come. To this day, fans and players alike feel great pride and confidence in their Trojans. USC baseball teams have won 11 national championships, more than any other Division I school. Trojans football teams have an all-time winning percentage of .700 and own a winning record against all conference opponents. USC football teams also have more Rose Bowl appearances and victories than any other school and have gone unbeaten in a season 14 times. This is a tradition rich in success and pride that has been built one year at a time.

TRAVELER, USC'S MASCOT

HORSE (ABOVE); LOS

ANGELES MEMORIAL

COLISEUM (BELOW)

ALL-PAC 10 PERFORMER DARRELL RUSSELL

THE TROJANS TRADITION

In the first decade of the 20th century, USC's football team forged ahead despite numerous limitations. Some years, the team had no coach; other years, it had no steady home field. The main problem, however, was always a lack of funding. The USC team found opponents wherever they could—local high schools, various Navy and National Guard teams, and USC alumni.

Until 1912, USC's athletic teams were called the Methodists or Wesleyans, but neither name was very popular with fans or university officials. So *Los Angeles Times* sports editor Owen Bird offered a suggestion.

"The term 'Trojan,'" Bird explained, "as applied to USC means to me that no matter what the situation, what the odds, or what the conditions, the completion must be carried on to the end and those who strive must give all they have and never be weary in doing so."

Southern California's teams never seemed to weary early in the century, posting eight consecutive winning seasons from 1903 to 1910. Bird's never-say-die nickname caught on, and by 1913, the name "Trojans" was official. After establishing their identity, the Trojans began to search for respect. Although the Pacific Coast Conference was formed in 1916 (USC joined in 1922), most of the attention in college football was focused on teams from the south, the midwest, and the east coast, who fought it out for the national title each year. But as the Trojans continued to battle, they began to earn more and more attention.

ROSE BOWLS AND RIVALRIES

In 1925, two years after the Trojans first played in their new stadium, the Los Angeles Memorial Coliseum, USC hired a new head coach: Howard Jones. In his earlier roles as head coach for Yale and then Iowa, Jones had built several national champions. Certainly, the Trojans knew what they were getting when they hired Jones—nothing less than a football wizard. But they got more than that. They got a dynasty.

Jones, a former defensive end at Yale, was a master at devising, training, and running strong, effective defenses. His practices emphasized blocking and tackling. "You have a spot about a yard or two on either side of you that nobody gets through," Jones said, explaining his simple philosophy on defensive line play. "No matter who winds up with the ball, they won't go anywhere."

In the late 1920s, Stanford was the west coast team to beat. Coached by the legendary Pop Warner, Stanford's innovative and flashy offensive formations had gained national acclaim by crushing such powerhouses as Notre Dame and Army. Teams all over the country were adopting Warner's strategies.

But Jones refused to embrace the Warner system, and in 1928, his Trojans shut out Warner's Stanford team 10–0. The Trojans' steady, disciplined defense wasn't fooled by Stanford's spins, draws, and fakes. The USC victory was particularly remarkable

OUTSTANDING HALFBACKS

AL CARMICHAEL (ABOVE) AND

DON GARLIN (BELOW, #29)

QUARTERBACK RODNEY PEETE WAS A DANGEROUS RUNNER.

because Stanford still had many of the players who had contributed to its national championship two years earlier. Supremacy on the west coast was passed from Warner to Jones as USC went on to win the national championship.

In 1929, with America about to slide headlong into the Great Depression, the Trojans played their cross-town rivals, the University of California, Los Angeles (UCLA), for the first time. Jones's "Thundering Herd," led by the breakaway running of quarterback Russ Saunders, put a 76–0 pasting on UCLA. The two teams played again the next year with similar results: the men of Troy won 52–0. Today, this rivalry is one of the most charged in all of organized sports.

In 1931, USC met Notre Dame in South Bend in front of a crowd of 52,000. The Fighting Irish were unbeaten in 26 straight games, but Jones's team was not intimidated.

Late in the third quarter, the Trojans found themselves down 14–0 but with the ball. USC's Orv Mohler took the ball right into the line and then spun around, tossing it back to left end Ray Sparling. Sparling knifed into the Irish defense, carrying the ball to the one-yard line. On the next play, Gus Shaver raced around the end to score the Trojans' first touchdown. Later, with only four minutes to play and the Irish leading 14–13, Shaver launched a 50-yard bomb to Sparling from his own 10, swinging the momentum back to the Trojans. USC then muscled into field goal range, and Johnny Baker booted the ball through the uprights as the stunned and silent crowd looked on. The climactic 16–14 Trojans win was only the second time Notre Dame had been defeated at home in 26 years.

FIERCE LINEBACKER JUNIOR

SEAU (ABOVE); QUARTERBACK

ROB JOHNSON (BELOW)

NAME: Howard Jones

BORN: August 23, 1885

DIED: July 27, 1941

POSITION: Head Coach

SEASONS COACHED: 1925–1940

AWARDS/HONORS: Three national championships, second-most coaching wins in USC history

RECORD: 121–36–13

During his 16-year tenure, Jones built USC into a dynasty. The former Yale player and coach was a master at building rock-solid defenses and running fundamentally sound offenses. The offense of his 1931 championship team scored a whopping 363 points, and the defense of his 1932 championship team gave up only 13 points the entire season. Jones turned the Trojans into one of the most feared and publicized teams in the nation. In 1940, he led his Trojans to a stunning 14–0 victory over powerful Tennessee in the Rose Bowl, snapping Tennessee's 23-game winning streak. The win, which came just one year before his death, gave Jones a perfect 5–0 career record in Rose Bowl games.

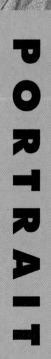

NAME: Frank Gifford

BORN: August 16, 1930

HEIGHT/WEIGHT: 6-foot-1/193 pounds

POSITION: Quarterback, defensive back, tailback

SEASONS PLAYED: 1949–1951

AWARDS/HONORS: All-American (1951), All-Pacific Coast Conference selection (1951), College Football Hall of Fame inductee

Gifford started his career as a quarterback and defensive back and was converted to tailback in his senior year, when he ran for 841 yards and was voted All-American. In his senior season, Gifford helped the Trojans topple then-top-ranked California on the Bears' home field. For his outstanding and versatile play, Gifford was inducted into the College Football Hall of Fame.

STATISTICS:

Season	Yards per pass	Touchdowns
1949	8.0	0
1950	3.8	0
	Rushing yards	Touchdowns
1951	841	7

The Trojans were national champions again, and the roots for another deep rivalry had been planted. The annual Irish-Trojan battle remains intense to this day.

WORLD WAR II AND BEYOND

After the Jones era, wins didn't come as easily for the men of Troy until the arrival of head coach Newell J. Cravath in 1942. Cravath was known as a tough and demanding coach who drilled and scrimmaged his teams exhaustively, often working them late into the night.

During World War II, Navy and Marine training programs were set up at USC. Cravath was able to recruit experienced players from these programs, and Trojans football thrived during the war years (1943–45), going 23–6–2 in that period.

Cravath led the Trojans to three straight Rose Bowl appearances. In 1944, USC blanked Washington 29–0 in the only matchup of west coast teams in Rose Bowl history. The Trojans also whitewashed Tennessee 25–0 in the 1945 Rose Bowl. But in 1946, against Alabama, USC fell 34–14. Although Alabama was a

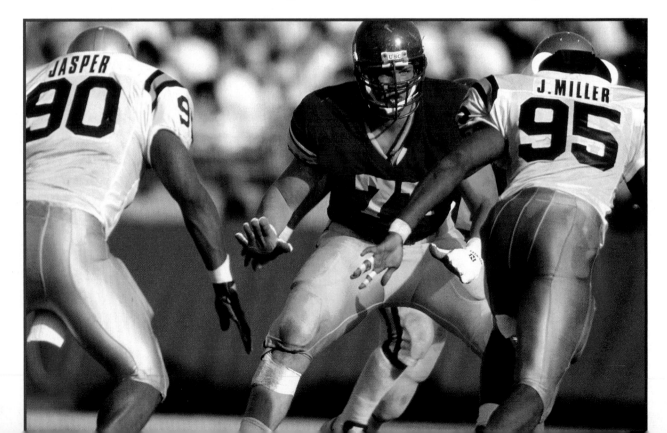

JUNIOR SEAU

powerhouse at the time, Trojans fans expected better. Said Braven Dyer of the *Los Angeles Times,* "Those of us who foolishly predicted Southern California's big linemen would wear down their lighter foes couldn't have guessed worse."

The Trojans suffered a more humiliating defeat when Michigan crushed them 49–0 in the 1948 Rose Bowl. It was the worst defeat in school history. That game triggered a three-year slide for USC, and Cravath's Trojans hung a 2–5–2 record in the books in 1950—Cravath's only losing season.

In 1951, Jesse T. Hill took over as coach and produced a winning team in his first year. The next year, he guided the Trojans back to the Rose Bowl, where they squeaked by Wisconsin 7–0 in a brutal defensive battle. Substitute quarterback Rudy Bukich tossed a 22-yard touchdown pass to Al "Hoagy" Carmichael in the third quarter for the only score of the game. Hill, who had played for the Trojans when they destroyed Pittsburgh 47–14 in the 1930 Rose Bowl, became the first man to have played on and coached winning Rose Bowl teams.

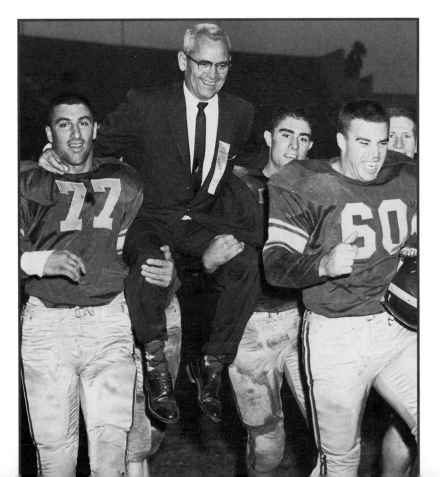

TAILBACKS AND COMEBACKS

In 1960, a new era began for Trojans football with the arrival of soon-to-be-legendary head coach John McKay. During his 15-year stint at USC, McKay would win 127 games and lose only 40. He would also reach the Rose Bowl eight times, and his Trojans teams would be named national champions four times.

McKay made his debut in the Rose Bowl in 1963, when his undefeated national champion team dodged an upset against the Wisconsin Badgers. Quarterback Pete Beathard threw four touchdown passes, and USC won in a shoot-out, 42–37.

McKay's I-formation offense created a legacy and some great tailbacks. Opposing coaches joked that McKay's playbook contained only two plays: student body right and student body left, so named because the Trojans would simply pitch the ball to their tailback and let him race to the corner behind a wall of pulling linemen. "With their big linemen coming around the corner, it always looked like USC had the whole student body blocking for

TAILBACK MIKE GARRETT

(ABOVE); ALL-AMERICAN

IRVINE "COTTON"

WARBURTON (BELOW)

COACH JOHN MCKAY

(ABOVE); HARD-

RUNNING BACK RICKY

BELL (BELOW)

their tailback, so that's what we called it," joked former UCLA head coach Terry Donahue.

McKay was also famous for putting a heavy workload on his runners, sometimes giving them 30 to 35 carries a game. When asked if he thought he was wearing out his talented backs, McKay responded, "I don't know why they would be tired. The ball ain't heavy." USC's first Heisman Trophy winner, Mike Garrett (1965), began the hard-working tradition. He set 14 NCAA, conference, and USC records in his three-year career, and later starred for the Kansas City Chiefs and San Diego Chargers in the National Football League.

O.J. Simpson, who won the Heisman Trophy in 1968 by the most one-sided vote in history, was a major factor in McKay's second national championship in 1967. "The Juice" ran for 1,543 yards that year, including 128 yards and two touchdowns in the Rose Bowl to lead the Trojans to a 14–3 victory over Indiana. Simpson went on to a brilliant 11-year NFL career.

Bruising fullback Sam "Bam" Cunningham, an All-American in 1972, was a human wrecking ball to opposing defenses. The 6-foot-3 and 215-pound back bulled for four touchdowns in the 1973 Rose Bowl against Ohio State, setting a Rose Bowl record. Cunningham's exploits broke open a game that had been tied 7–7 at halftime, and USC rode his coattails to a 42–17 blowout.

After Cunningham came Anthony Davis and Ricky Bell. Both were runners-up in Heisman voting. Davis, an All-American in 1974, led the Trojans in rushing for three years. Bell, a two-time All-American, once rushed for 347 yards against Washington State in 1976. His USC teammates called him "Mad Dog" and growled whenever he carried the ball.

In 1974, Davis and Bell helped the Trojans engineer what is still regarded as one of the most incredible comebacks in the history of college football. Notre Dame was trouncing the Trojans 24–0 late in the first half. Because Notre Dame's defense was ranked number one in the nation, things looked especially bleak for USC. But with 10 seconds remaining in the quarter, USC's Rhodes scholar quarterback Pat Haden completed a seven-yard swing pass to Davis for a touchdown. The Trojans went to the locker room behind 24–6, but there was hope.

Davis caught the second-half kickoff, cut behind a block by Bell, and raced 102 yards down the left sideline to score. Davis scored again three minutes later on a short run; and three minutes after that, he added another touchdown and a two-point conversion to make it 27–24, USC. But the Trojans didn't stop there. Haden connected twice with his best friend and high school teammate Johnny McKay for touchdowns, and the Trojans were up 41–24 as the third quarter ended. A fumble recovery and an interception led to two more scores that finally ended the scoring explosion at 55–24. USC had scored its 55 points in less than 17 minutes.

"We turned into madmen," Davis said after the game. Indeed, the Trojan comeback was frenzied and inspired. Haden

ANTHONY DAVIS RAN FOR 1,421 YARDS AND 18 TOUCHDOWNS IN 1974.

NAME: Marcus Allen

BORN: March 26, 1960

HEIGHT/WEIGHT: 6-foot-2/200 pounds

POSITION: Tailback

SEASONS PLAYED: 1978–81

AWARDS/HONORS: All-American (1981), 1981 Pac-10 Player of the Year, 1981 Heisman Trophy winner

Allen brought USC its fourth Heisman Trophy in 1981, when he became the first player in college football history to rush for more than 2,000 yards in a season. A smart, elusive runner with surprising strength, Allen was also a dependable receiver coming out of the backfield. He finished his career with an NCAA-record 11 games with at least 200 rushing yards.

STATISTICS:

Season	Rushing yards	Touchdowns
1978	171	1
1979	649	8
1980	1,563	14
1981	2,342	23

NAME: R. Jay Soward

BORN: January 16, 1978

HEIGHT/WEIGHT: 5-foot-11/175 pounds

POSITION: Wide receiver, kick returner

SEASONS PLAYED: 1996–

AWARDS/HONORS: All-Pac-10 honorable mention selection (1996), All-Pac-10 second-team selection (1997, 1998)

Explosive and multitalented, Soward proved to be USC's big-play weapon and one of college football's most exciting play-makers as a freshman in 1996. Each of his seven touchdowns went an average of 66 yards. The speedster continued to whirl through defenses in 1997 and 1998 as a receiver, runner, and kick and punt returner. "He's one of the great receivers I've seen," legendary coach Lou Holtz said.

STATISTICS:

Season	Yards per reception	Touchdowns
1996	28.2	7
1997	17.3	11
1998	15.4	6

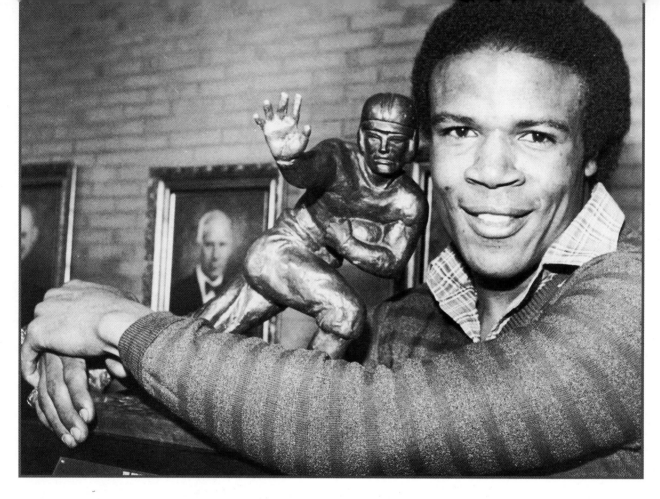

connected on eight of eight passes, Davis scored 26 points, and McKay—son of coach McKay—had four catches, two for touchdowns.

The magic of the Notre Dame game stuck with the Trojans as they met Ohio State in the Rose Bowl for the third straight year. USC trailed the Buckeyes 17–10 with just two minutes left to play when Haden completed a 38-yard pass to McKay in the end zone to draw within one. Haden then hit a diving Shelton Diggs on the two-point conversion to give Southern California another dramatic, last-minute victory and the national title.

THE ROBINSON YEARS

After the 1975 season, McKay left USC to become the head coach of the NFL's Tampa Bay Buccaneers. His successor, John Robinson, kept USC on the winning track. He led the Trojans to an 11–1 record and a 14–6 victory in the 1977 Rose Bowl against Michigan, becoming only the second rookie coach from the Pac-8 Conference to capture a Rose Bowl. In that game, freshman tailback Charles White filled in for the injured Ricky Bell and ran for 122 yards and a touchdown. Another USC coach was on his way to legendary status, and the tradition of outstanding tailbacks continued.

Charles White went on to become USC's third Heisman Trophy winner, racking up a conference-record 6,245 career yards. The Trojans won back-to-back Rose Bowls in 1979 and 1980, and White was named Player of the Game in each contest. The 1980 game was an intense battle with Ohio State. With 5:21 remaining on the clock and the Buckeyes up 16–10, USC got the ball on their own 17. Then White took control. USC hammered their way 83 yards down the field, all on the ground, for a touchdown. On the winning drive, White stole the show, carrying the ball six times for 71 yards.

In 1981, college football saw its first 2,000-yard rusher: USC's fourth Heisman Trophy winner, Marcus Allen. Not only did Allen set 14 new NCAA records for rushing, but he also caught 30

RODNEY PEETE (ABOVE)

AND JOHN ROBINSON

(BELOW) PLAYED IN

ROSE BOWLS.

and 34 passes in his last two seasons. Allen went on to have a magnificent career in the NFL with the Los Angeles Raiders and Kansas City Chiefs.

Robinson's tenure came to a close after the 1982 season, and his last game was a controversial, comeback victory over rival Notre Dame. With 48 seconds left on the clock, Trojans tailback Michael Harper appeared to have fumbled as he dove across the goal line, but the touchdown counted, and USC prevailed 17–13.

The win put Robinson's career record at 67–14–1.

Throughout Robinson's coaching term, his teams were ranked in the top 20 for all but two weeks, including a six-week stretch in 1979 at number one.

THE CENTURY MARK

After a few mediocre years, the Trojans put together a string of winning seasons from 1987 to 1990. The last game of the 1987 season was a stunning upset against heavily-favored UCLA. Southern California was down 13–0 in the third quarter, but in typical fashion, the Trojans put another amazing comeback victory in the history books. A juggling, corner-of-the-end-zone catch by Erik Affholter from Rodney Peete put USC up for good late in the game.

ALL-AMERICAN TONY

BOSELLI (ABOVE);

THE SWIFT JUNIOR

SEAU (BELOW)

"We were supposed to have no chance—none," recalled safety Mark Carrier, who intercepted two of Bruins quarterback Troy Aikman's passes. "They were bigger, faster, stronger. But we had Rodney."

The win put USC in the Rose Bowl, but the Trojans lost the big game to Michigan State 20–17 in spite of two Rodney Peete touchdown passes in the second half. Peete finished second in the Heisman voting that year behind standout Oklahoma State running back Barry Sanders.

USC faced Michigan in the Rose Bowl the following year, and Michigan came back from a 14–3 halftime deficit to win 22–14. The loss spoiled the finale of USC's 100th anniversary of football. Again, Peete put in a remarkable performance, running for a pair of touchdowns. But the normally stubborn Trojans defense, led by future San Diego Chargers All-Pro linebacker Junior Seau, couldn't prevent Rose Bowl MVP Leroy Hoard from rumbling for 142 yards and two touchdowns of his own.

After two Rose Bowl disappointments in a row, USC coach Larry Smith was fiercely determined to reverse the fortunes of his program. "It is not a big deal here at USC to merely make it to the Rose Bowl," stated Smith. "It's only a big deal here when you win it." Luckily for Smith, the third time was the charm. The Trojans earned their third consecutive trip to the Rose Bowl in 1990 and

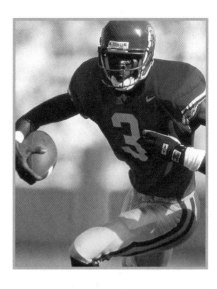

TALENTED RECEIVERS

KEYSHAWN JOHNSON

(ABOVE) AND JOHNNIE

MORTON (BELOW)

outlasted the Wolverines for a 17–10 win. The game-winning score came with 1:10 left to play as tailback Ricky Ervin scampered 14 yards for a touchdown, capping a 75-yard drive.

THE '90S

The 1980s had proven to be a time of great ups and downs for the Trojans, and after unimpressive seasons in 1991 and 1992, the school rehired proven winner John Robinson. By the final week of his first season back, the team was nationally ranked again.

The Trojans appeared in their 28th Rose Bowl after the 1995 season, matched up against number-three ranked Northwestern. The Wildcats had surprised the nation by posting their first winning record since 1971 and making their first bowl game appearance since 1949. But the Trojans' no-huddle offense and the spectacular play of wide receiver Keyshawn Johnson put an end to Northwestern's Cinderella season. USC quarterback Brad Otton shredded Northwestern's secondary, completing 29 of 44 passes for 391 yards, two touchdowns, and no interceptions. Trojans cornerback Daylon McCutcheon added a 53-yard fumble return for a touchdown as USC outgunned the Wildcats, 41–32.

USC won only six games in 1996. A sluggish offense and an erratic defense sabotaged the Trojans' hopes of rising once again

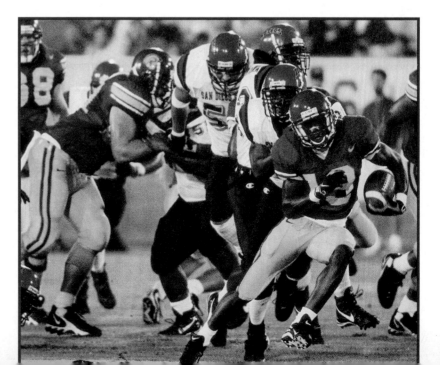

1998 ALL-AMERICAN CHRIS CLAIBORNE

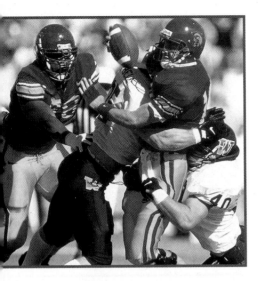

BRAD OTTON (ABOVE)

AND DAYLON MCCUTCHEON

(BELOW) LED THE TROJANS

IN THE '90S.

to the top of the national rankings. Change was needed, and, after the 1997 season, Robinson was fired to make way for USC alum Paul Hackett. As the new head coach, Hackett brought enthusiasm and an impressive coaching resume to the table. He had served as an assistant coach for USC in the late 1970s and had also worked in the NFL for the Dallas Cowboys and Kansas City Chiefs.

Hackett was looking to tune up a sputtering USC attack with the play of quarterback Mike Van Raaphorst and multitalented offensive threat R. Jay Soward. The Trojans' talented and deep defense, led by strong safety David Gibson, should continue to be among the best in the nation.

"It's an honor and a privilege to have this job," said Hackett at the press conference announcing his hiring. "USC football owns a special place in my heart and in the hearts of our fans across the country. My goal is to take this program back to the level where it belongs: among the best in the country."

The Trojans faithful hope that with an injection of new coaching blood, the days of big-game heroics and national championships will return to Southern California. Then, once again, the warning cry, "Beware the men of Troy!" will be heard all across the land.